baby, sweetheart, honey

Emily Perkovich

abuddhapress@yahoo.com

Alien Buddha Press 2023

®™©

Emily Perkovich 2023

ISBN: 978-1-959118-15-2

···Contents···

Foreword, kind of

I can't speak for anywhere else in the world but being anything but a cis-het white male in America is becoming increasingly difficult. It has never been easy. There was this small amount of time where it seemed like we were operating under these minuscule steps of progress. It felt like we were climbing two flights of stairs and then taking an elevator down to the previous floor—to expound on the two steps forward one step back adage. At some point that elevator started plummeting several floors at a time, and even with our feet pounding to make it to the next floor up, we are never moving anywhere but down, let alone making it to the penthouse. And did I mention that the basement is on fire, so the heat is increasing to climb back up with each fall? I'm saying that society is declining in more ways than I know how to quantify, but especially on a civil and humanitarian level.

Looking around at our neighbors, this doesn't seem to be an issue unique to America. The only real difference is that America has been shouting for so long about how progressive we are, that we have shrouded our oppression under echoes that are still louder than our cries for help. The reverb of celebration over the smallest victories in equality is so amplified that even people here witnessing it are not able to see and hear how quick this decline has been.

I am terrified to be a woman here. I am terrified to be a person who is comfortable with my sexuality and with speaking out about it as frequently as I do. I don't even feel that I can trust other women now, unless they have experienced similar traumas to my own, and sometimes even then, they seem to have undergone some type of conversion therapy to make them numb to the suffering that is bearing down on us all. I'm so tired of witnessing the judgement of what and how you are allowed to do, say, wear, feel, react, and cope to any situation or trauma. Especially from people forming those opinions from a place of ignorance. And I don't even mean that in the negative, stigmatized way. I mean if you aren't trying to be educated on something, then I think most people don't want or need your opinion on the matter because a lot of the time it can be extremely harmful to healing and coping.

This collection is in no way comprehensive, because I don't want to play the savior for everyone else. I want to be clear about the fact that I am speaking from a sexually fluid, slightly promiscuous, white, female identifying, atheist mother's perspective (there are probably other labels I could throw in there, but these seem to be the ones that may shape my opinions and experiences the most), but I do believe that the majority of these experiences are being shared between anyone and everyone that is not part of the ruling class of straight, white, misogynist men, and we all need to be better and more empathetic to each other. I say this so frequently online, in forewords, in blurbs and reviews, and day to day in person, but we need to start being informed on feelings and reactions. Just knowing that people experience hardships is not enough to start making more empathetic choices. For so many generations, we weren't supposed to feel or react (unless it was with white-man rage) to anything. That is not only unhealthy, but it creates so much stigma around situations and reactions that are actually commonplace, that people are afraid to talk about anything because they might be judged. To exacerbate that, people don't feel comfortable expressing their emotions, so it would stand to reason they aren't going to feel comfortable expressing the emotions they feel when they are being judged for feeling. It's a circle that creates silence, when we need to be talking and discussing what is really happening.

All of that being said, this collection deals with the fear and traumas that I have experienced as a woman (connected to all those aforementioned labels) in this country. Content warnings cover sexually explicit language, behavior, and violence, domestic violence, miscarriage, mention of abortion procedures, suicide, self-harm, religious trauma, eating disorders, class trauma, and toxic friendships

♥
—Emily Perkovich

False Advertising

/two inches below thighs/whole inch above fingertips/

this is the hot spot where we tattoo our women with "take me, if hem falls above this line" just under the intersection of "asking for it" & "open for business"

/if you need a visual, drop a pin an inch south of "property of men"/

because someone marked the whole goddamn vessel as "for sale" at birth.

your male-god pulled me from ribcage, so it's only natural for you to prod and poke/to dig your fingers into the wet earth of me/when you need a reminder of what it feels like to breathe.

/don't forget you still need a woman to teach you to breathe/

to be born in these bodies is to be made an open invitation, rsvp unnecessary. because when you crowned, they took you from the throne of your mother and handed you off to man. and somehow, as mothers, we still haven't learned to believe the abducted. we still think the wanted poster a lie. we still think the missing will be found.

/to be born a woman, is to be born missing/

do you remember when your god didn't believe you about the snake?

do you remember what it's like when no one believes you?

Visiting Regrets

My ribs shake with the things I am not
Collarbones crack
I practice locking doors
It's the flutter at the wrists
The hairline-flush
I break the bowls
But I'd still eat an excuse from your palm
You place blame in the spot that leaves you innocent
I place myself between your breaths and imagine myself as an inhale
Know I am always the exhale

It's Funny How I Always Run Out Of Steam By The End Of The Poem

It's in the center of a neon lock falling closed that I realize disdain

It's unfortunate to love you through the hate, and my stomach is twisting, and I'm dizzy on the smell of mid-summer refracting off your skin, mid-day, mid-show, mid-song, mid-throw, and your head bounces off the grass, and I help you to your feet, before I notice the match, notice the key

Mention here: the break down

I'm cutting my hair in the hotel shower, running through muscle deterioration, I'm hiding the pill bottle in the deep pocket, so it's harder to reach in sleep fugues, I'm making my story private, but you're still screaming me, me, me, against the Chicago winds

But it's true. I know I was raped, but you were raped too, and here's where I mention how your rape is the one that matters

Mention here: her rape was the one that mattered

Look, I'm suicidal, and I'm throwing up in airport bathrooms, and my grandfather is dead, and I'm debating if I have the fortitude to start snorting, and I'm sorry, because they're passing abortion bans, and they're electing men, and me caring about my rights is a trigger for your pain, and your grandfather is dead too, and so I'm sorry, and I'm removing the men, and I'm removing the other women, and I'm removing myself from your fucking equation, because it's easier to count me out, and I'm a fistful of pills, and you're an unanswered text, and I'm figuring out how to stop mentioning it, and I mention it here, I mention

Mention here: it's ok if you're not ok, if it doesn't affect her, and if her being ok is your priority

And if you listen close to this flashback, you realize how you're not the only one who abandoned me, I'm abandoning myself, so that way there's less blame for you, because you're the priority here, you're putting yourself first, you're setting boundaries, you're eliminating distraction, you're calling me safe house while you lock the door and set me on fire

Mention here: burning it down

Do you remember how I promised I'd burn it down? Do you remember how you burned us down? You call a mother a dragon, and I never realized I was the surrogate, I swallow your fire, realize this is the moment when I burn myself down

The Ballad of Maddy and Cassie

—After Marisa Silva-Dunbar

White, pigtail-baby hanging on queen's skirt for scraps, porcelain-doll Cassie turning carnival circles, riding her candy-carousel orgasms, blue-eyed preening for sloppy seconds from the high school king of brooding, king of explosion, king of the gaslight, king of the narcissists

Maddy knew, Maddy didn't need the man, Maddy the only monologue that matters, Maddy literally going to get violent, Maddy oh you're crying? Maddy you fucking bitch.

Maddy hand-plucking her sister, soul-mating the bitch, Cassie hand-plucking Maddy's heart, becoming the bitch, betraying the bitch

Maddy glitters, becomes the knife blade
Cassie fades, becomes the mirror

5

you named me mother, and i was naïve enough to watch you slit the
throat of the one who birthed you, to burn the one who raised you,
yet still imagine i'd teach you table manners, i nursed you through
your tongue-tie, let your gums gnash nipples raw, i never saw it
coming, the way you'd refuse to wipe your mouth as i watched
myself drip down your chin, how you'd claim you'd kissed teeth

I Write Myself Into Your Shoes
And Change The Setting

I come to in the thick of it
Find you face down in flooded fields
I imagine you as me

we're face to face mixing breath, we're skin to skin mixing signals, I brush
fingers on hips, watch the way your words come out whispered in the negative,
know this is the moment when things snap, you're on the ground as I push my
heel into neck, limbs scrambling as I roll you stomach-bound, press my palm
to back of head, you're screaming, and I'm watching the mud fill the gaps in
your teeth, watching browned grass catch in your throat, I laugh, call you
water-logged, dig a trench across you, spike your spine, till the surface

I come to in the thick of it
Open the window on the scene
Flash freeze the field
You bleed dirt from all your holes
Scream again for an ending

Portrait of a Fever

Epidermis flushes, concrete drips dizzy with heat
I wish for the ache to dislodge, for the skin to burn raw
I wish I could count how many ways to say it hurts
I wish I knew where it hurts
I pick through the bile to dredge up the scabs
Peel back the softened layers
You imagine it crimson
Gummy tissue rotting to bruise
I bleed only in still frames of beds
The sheets are still virgins
The rays wash out all color

And I flush
       And I drip
             O, how I drip

We're Getting a Divorce, You Keep the Dishes

You are ill at ease—and my discomfort only grows. And the swelling, it fills. It bursts. It rattles. Explodes. Explodes. And I may be sugary-sweet. But I am hot-lava, black cake. Contain me, you won't. Charred, raw, melting. Catch me in your kitchen at midnight. Barefoot, exposed. Moonlit, soft. And I will slowly break the bowls if it means new vessels are coming. Contain me, you won't. These don't quite fit my shape. For I am sleepy-sweet, energy-spent. Post-explosion ruptured. Crescendo, crescendo. It is midnight, and I am pulling glass from shelves. Throwing ceramics to floor in upsurge of shards. Intestinal-fits. Guts, been-exposed. Let my insides out. Building, building. And I am destroying dishes. I am spinning plates for fun. I am shattering the things that hold us. Lunar-light on sharpened threshold. Glitter, glimmer. Catapult-collision, floor and glass. The apex. The apex. Let me spill. Contain me, you won't.

THE MATCH THAT SET THE HOUSE ON FIRE

I FEEL THE GHOST OF EVERY HAND THAT WAS EVER
SWATTED AWAY.
I FEEL EVERY FINGER
THAT CRAWLED INSIDE ME
FEIGNING MISUNDERSTANDING.
I FEEL MYSELF FULL WITH WHAT I DID NOT ASK FOR.
FULL WITH DISAGREEMENT,
POURING OUT MY BLOODIED, RAW THROAT.
FULL WITH THE WORDS PINNING ME DOWN.
AND FULL WITH FIRE AT THE REALIZATION THAT THERE
WAS TRUTH NAUGHT BEHIND THE WORDS.
FULL WITH FIRE, BRIMMING OVER.
FULL WITH FIRE, POOLING BETWEEN MY LEGS.
FLAMES LICKING MY THIGHS.
LASHING IN HOT BREATHS
AT EACH HAND THAT DARES
AFTER BEING SWATTED.
WHIPPING AND SCORCHING
THE CREEPING FINGERTIPS.
ENVELOPING ME FULL.
AND BURNING THE WORDS AWAY INTO CHARRED RUINS.
AND THE GHOSTS DO NOT LEAVE.
I CARRY THEM WITH ME.
BUT I NO LONGER CARRY THE BLAME.
THAT
BELONGS TO YOU.
AND YOU SPARKED AN INFERNO WHEN YOU TRIED TO
PLACE IT INSIDE OF ME.

WELCOME TO YOUR PRIVATE BONFIRE.
TONIGHT
FOR ONCE,
WE WILL BURN
you
AT THE STAKE.

20

Becoming the Lilliputian

I become obsessed with the word cunt/how the c clicks at the roof of the mouth, hugs the other letters in strong arms, how the u is a wet-pussy smile, and the n the perfect teasing, rhythmic shape, i use the t to split myself in half, prepare for a drowning/i buy my fingers a new outfit, drape velvet to knuckles, apply black polish like mascara/i'm dressed to thrill, to kill, to spill, dressed to fill/i spread like a starfish, two fingers as legs, two fingers as arms, one finger as mouth, five fingers come crawling/i am an opening, a hole, an empty shadow/i push at damp flesh, lick sticky entrance, come-hither my way to deep pink/i dance a slippery waltz across boundaries, clench tight around heart, ignite the wick at both ends/the fire burns through/i'm pulling out intestines as i find salvation

Wild One Likes the Wild Ones

wild one grows up too fast, sees too much, wild one dances in the streets and sleeps on the beach, wild one, wild one, wild one eats rarely, sleeps rarely, speaks rarely, wild one holds her tongue rarely, wild one grows up too fast, but only the first time, wild one can't think through the haze, wild one doesn't want the haze, wild one throws fists, not second, but first, wild one holds hands, pushes away, don't touch her there, wild one says don't touch her there, then lets you touch her there, wild one is a blood-letting, wild one is a bonfire, wild one is a controlled burn, a rampant flood, wild one is stuck in the haze, wild one grows up again, grows roots in pavement, spins wheels against pavement, wild one lets you hold her in the back seat, wild one is a hole shaped like the back seat, wild one leaves her clothes easily, wild one hates her body, loves that you love her body, wild one grows up again, wild one is a smoke signal, wild one swallows smoke signals, wild one is begging for a smoke signal, wild one watches her youth float across the smoke signals, wild one dips her toes in the waves, wild one climbs the rocks, lets you pull her up the rocks, wild one watches you throw her from your rocks, wild one still can't eat, still can't sleep, still can't speak, touches too much, likes to feel too much, wild one, wild one, wild one waits for you to touch too much, wild one says hold her down, wild one holds herself down, wild one is holding it all down, when wild one grows up again, grows alone, grows lonely, loves you feral, still misses you feral, wild one wants a purge, wild one is on her knees, wild one begs you to swallow her whole, misses you feral, wishes for you wild and feral, wild one reaches for the ground, is one foot in the grave, is tip-toe, chin-up, head just barely above ground, both feet in the grave, digging for the gravel of whispered words, wild one is a grave digger, wild one is digging her own grave, wild one is covering her grave, wild one is buried in the gravel of whispered words, growing up too fast, growing up again, growing up again, wild one, growing up again, again

Something Black & Blue

I wore bruises to my wedding.
No dress.
I wore my blood as chains around my wrists.
I wore a pregnant belly and dark circles beneath my eyes.
I wore my hopelessness like a scarlet letter.
I wore my white flag of surrender.
I wore ink on paper as a prison cell.
There was never any dress.

May Crowning

Dry earth splits with repulsion
There is a paradox in the crying shame that a dehydrated cell forgets how to
soak
It's a crying shame that any devil can conceive an awakening
I'm comparing swelling to an eviction
                          There is a paradox to—
I never wanted an open plot until one was thrust upon me
I watched an orchid blossom beneath the hem of my skirt
                          And I'll tell you what
It's in the petals unfurling that I fall in love
A tendril scrapes me clean
And, I do
I fall in love
I am the chasm
I am the crimson rush we love to forget
I am in love with the building up of an orchid
                          Until all I want is open plots
Twelve summers can tarnish the bed
                          And I'll tell you what
A finger buds slower than an atrium
I water the blooms with a blood-letting
                          Next summer, there's always next summer
And still the new orchids weep

D&C

My mom used to work in hospitals and nursing homes. Long shifts. Heavy lifting. Clean-up in Room 3. Spilled-guts. Spilled-bowels. Spilled-bladder. Spilled-blood. Human-spill. Spill-spillage. She'd come home to house, nighttime-still. She'd come home to pass-out, lack of sleep. Stumble down stairs, wash away fluids. Wash away E. Coli. Wash away sweat. Wash away death-stench. Pass-out lack of sleep. Repeat, next day. Lift-up crying. Lift-up disease. Lift-up dying. Lift-up human-spillage. Repeat. Lift-up human-spillage. Repeat. The babies never had a chance. Twins. Fallopian-tube, burst. Platelet, internal-vein explosion. Ghost-bleeding. Phantom-bleeding. Insides-bleeding. Also known as hemorrhage. Also known as dying. Also known as 8 hours screaming/fainting/shaking pain. Also known as doctor-induced abort mission. Ride or die. Abort mission or sleep-eternal. No blood left. So I could hold two still-borns. One mass explosion. The other clump of tadpole-mess. Save the unborn. Send the living home. Follow the plan. Return home. Spare the rod, spoil the child. Kill the mother, spare the child. Or spoon-scrape cervix. Tissue-removal. Tissue-removal. And I wake every day thanking the doctor that left her blood-cup-half-full. Pray to false god of saving lives. Return me home. Return me home.

why i'll always be haunted

i.

hands
too many hands, touching all the wrong spots. too much pressure, in places
that never asked to be stained with dirty fingerprints and filthy mouths.

ii.

nights i woke up blindfolded. nights i woke up deaf. nights i woke up
screaming. nights i woke up dead. nights i never slept.

iii.

the way the refrigerator felt pressed up against my back. anorexic-spine refusing
to bend and break. chin up, tears checked. the way that the solid object gave
false confidence. the way my bones still cracked.

iv.

the wedding ring in the grass.

v.

tubes & wires
small lungs failing. because babies don't belong here this early. but trauma has a
way of bringing out the best of us.

vi.

tubes & wires
"you can't hold him."
"please give me back my baby?"
"you have nerve damage."
"give me my baby back!"
"someone put her back to sleep."

vii.

distance and space and sirens and screams. and how all of those words just feel like the word abandoned. and how everyone always leaves.

viii.

all these fucking metaphors.

ix.

my wrists tied to his knuckles. and how he hangs around my neck. and how he hangs around my thoughts. and how he gets hung up in my throat. and how my eyes feel hung out to dry.

x.

the way the mirror explodes when it sees my face. how two of my fingers fit so perfectly at the back of my mouth. how i reach for the devil and up comes the ache.

Drunken Blizzards

Her head presses against cool glass, stomach still turning. She doesn't know why, but one of his favorite games is scaring them. Too many drinks and too late in the night, he pulled the three girls from the party. He woke her violent from her already restless sleep. Too many drinks and a loud, showy repeat of a previous fight. All eyes on him. And him, voice blasting across the party. And mama pulls at his wrist, but he can't even feel her there. He's all name calling and feet stomping. Broken bottles and cards strewn across the floor. And she's all forced laughs, begging, and pleading. Because nothing is wrong. And none of them have ever seen a storm. And nothing is wrong. And he yanks them all past the whispers and pushes them into the car. And too many people watch from the driveway as the car screeches away into the night. Too many drinks, and too cold a night, and he purposefully throws the car in dizzying, lurching circles. Snowbanks dislodge and explode outside her window as the tires tread them, too quick. And she mustn't cry. Her mama is crying. Her sister is crying. But she mustn't cry. If she doesn't cry, the storm will never come. And so she lets the glass ease her turning stomach. And when he asks if she thinks it's funny, she stares straight into his eyes, silent, wordless. And he laughs like they're party to a private joke. And she rests her head back against the glass. And she watches the snow rise and fall again like it's been given a second chance to hit the ground. And she thinks how life is always just repeating. Pounding, angry snowfalls turning to dirty piles, too heavy to hold. And her mama is crying. And her sister is crying. And he's still shouting and laughing. Great, joyous cries whooping into the bright, white night. And a little prick of her fear slips away as she realizes there's no stopping the storms. And she can't help but to laugh at the joke as well.

A Reaping, A Sowing

I visit my grave, again
Refuse to kneel
I track the mud across the floor, again
Refuse to kneel

I cull
I prune
Sunbathe the plot
Flood the burial
The flowers never grow

I tear a petal from the stamen, hold a heart in my right hand, lungs in my left,
this one says I love me, this one says not, and it's that familiar feeling again,
everything ends with rot

I bury flowers slowly

Fingerprints are pushing through earth, rising to surface, reaching for solidity,
never full-fledged hands

I'm burying girl parts

Brush dirt from the folds

The flowers never grow

i don't know how to hold pretty things

we watch a boy say incandescent and he means you are and i think how to apply that and she notates the quality but then all i come up with is luminescent and i worry that this is how internal wars start the pin drops in front of the loaded gun of the church mouse and i remember that silence rhymes with violence

do you remember your first kiss

i ate the tongue of a boy from the quarry
we kept hands at sides
stood chest to chest
scruffy mouth scraping my cupid's bow with friction
he licked his lips at release

i do not remember my first kiss

a boy held me close in science hall
freckled face sang me spanish lullabies
i watched him finger pick my ribs
callouses climbing collarbones
and maybe i remember his melody

but i don't remember that kiss either

i bathe in incandescence, swim in clarity, transcend into fever dreams, a hand creeps up my uniform skirt, a hand presses the back of head, a hand pushes me rough into a janitors' closet, a hand at my cunt, a hand in my mouth, i choke on how incandescent the throat of a shadow remains

Fits & Bursts, Bits & Pieces

I remember the checkerboard floor
The story goes you inhaled the crotch of my 8-year-old panties
I never learned chess
I hear sights
The bulb blinks against my eardrums
I'm haunted by a double-wide
The canopy was only shielding your mouth
I press my skin against the web and you both thrum, electric
The canopy never shields my body
I take swimming lessons in the bath and drown in a stolen youth
I'm over-exposed
I'm half-light
I'm muted, spun in spider silk
I belt the notes louder than the engine
You slam feet
Crack my skull like you mean it

Chapter 3: The Things That Lawyers Never Tell

I write all the handprints bloody
even though we both know that
cadavers don't bleed,

bloody the gums, bloody the
teeth, bloody the scene,

cradle the receiver in blood, the
mouthpiece in blood, bloody
fingerprints on the dial tone
fading into bloodied silence,

we've been here before, your dna
is never on the evidence, but mine
is always all over your hands when
I release you from custody, I don't
need a trial to know the verdict is
in your favor, you're the blind-jury
in your own courtroom-head, I
apologize and pay your bail, drop
the charges, crawl home,

bloody the knees

DMs

No disrespect but. I want you to milk me, I will pay if it is good like I
imagine

God I'm going to fuck u

Lmu? I'll pay

Hi, can you answer? Don't be bitxh

Pls chat with me

Did you get my picture? I'm throbbing

Can I get a rating?

What that mouth do, lol

Babe did you read my mssg, I need to know what size plug you can take

I love your jiggly thighs with a tight ass

Damn, mama

Mom I'd like to fuck me lmao

You like when I make my girlfriend bitch watch?

Fucking bjtxh

Fuck you

I want to fuck that tight pink pussy.

All them tats? You a masochist? You kinky like that?

I want to break yiur skin

Send pics?

Fuck!

Goddamn

I wanna fuck that mouth

Please forgive me for what I'm about to say, I'd love to go down on you kiss
lick and suck on your sweet pussy clit and ass for an hour or longer and just
watch your facial expressions and listen to the sounds you'd be making

So hot, kinky, tease. Send more , but free tits and asshole

Do you want to see the penis?

Next time you post a tease I will fuck you until you bleed

Yeah baby you want that thick cock. Send me a voice clip moaning.

Let me lick that drippy cunt

Fuck me

God I want to fuck you

Are you looser after kids? If so I'll need the asshole

Dear, pls answe

You just fucking want money

I will spread you til it hurts

Fat bitch with small tits

I want to break your jaw apart with my dick

I'm biting your nipples and my cock slips into your ass

I'm going to fuck your ass until you shit and then I make you lick my dick

Babe, you're making me hard

But why you no a squirter? I'm not pay for no squirting.

Your tattoos make me cum

Can I use you for my art?

Puke on my dick, dirty girl!

Baby, I want to give you rope burn

You are imaging, I spread you open, tongue slips in slit, you drip into your own ass, I shove my fingers in two knuckles and I circle your clit, and you want me so much and I will not untie you because we are edging and I will never let you cum and so I push my cock into your mouth until I feel it is hot at the back of your throat and your so sexy and I push your head into my shaft and explode but you still cant cum

Prostitute

I want to lick between your toes while you're tied down and can't escape

No thinking. Just enjoy my force.

Cunt

Bitch!

Bet you stink though!!!!!

Baby, I just drooled on my cock thinking of your pussy

I want to hurt you

Your not a sugar baby just gold digging cunt

I'll pay 2k a week for just talk dirty, no nudes, just make me cum

Fuckkkkkkk

Babe, I wanna bust it on that pretty face

Lemme smoke in that pussy hole

Don't wanna reply? Or to busy with other stuff or people??

Cant decide if your nipples or pussy excite me more

pussy looks delicious, want to lick on suck on those beautiful pussy lips and clit, then replace that plug with my tongue..

I want to ask you a thing, when I fkkk you will you cry around my dick?

I truly love your perfect shaped ass

I forgot my password. Just snd free pics please?

we can see that absolutely gorgeous perfect amazing pussy

Butt plugs are my fave! You've got me so thick right nowwwwwwww

Hello, would you like to try drp with me? Please, free pls

Pussysoyummy pusyyummmmmmy

I want to spread you pussy as wide as this mouth of yours

Y u not let me drink your milk, mommy

I want to fuck you.

I want fuck you..

I fuck u?

When we fuck?

I want to fuck you!

Damn so sexyyyy

Guess you're not interested sorry to have bothered you

4.4.22

I don't remember how to pick myself out of a lineup.
I scatter parts like sowing seeds.
The failure is in the lack of growth.
It's spring, but nothing's bloomed, save the crocus.
I do not know how to blush in shades of violet.
I split under the ice.
Color myself permafrost.
I've been searching for a thaw but breaking against the solidity.

I keep throbbing in beds, I never really left. I wish I could say I was wrapped in satin. I'm cocooned in cotton. I'm stripped under falling snow. Confusing the season's arrival for a nightmare ending. I'm unclothed, hard body pushed against my back. I'm sweat pooling between knees and elbows, dripping from hairline. I'm freezing beneath open windows, with fight or flight heat thrumming beneath the surface. I'm sick of mouths kissing me in my sleep. I'm sick of hands at my neck in my sleep. I'm sick of fingers between my thighs in my sleep. I'm sick of palms pushing my face into the mattress in my sleep. I'm sick of sleeping with his hands finding me dry, and his hands wrapping around my stomach, and his hands pushing my hair behind my ears, and his hands throwing me to the floor, and his hands spreading my legs apart, and his hands pushing inside of me, and his hands thrusting his cock inside of me, and his hands letting go so his cock can find my ass, and my hands clawing at the wooden floors, and my hands bound under my ribs, and my hands catching vomit in the palm, and my hands held in his, and my hands convinced his hands made a mistake, my hands penning excuses, my hands penning a misunderstanding, my hands comforting my betrayal, and my hands hot and shaking, and I'm sick of shaking, and it's spring, it's not winter.

And I once blushed in shades of violet.
But I'm sick of hands forcing me into violet.

What You Stole from Me

I remember our skin pressed together, hot, at seventeen. I remember long nights in your basement room. Lazy days in my bed behind a locked door. I remember the sun bringing your freckles out to play and toasting my skin to your favorite shade of me. I remember your fingers creeping inside of me playful on train rides to the city. Your mouth sleepy on my own and your arms pulling me into the cradle of dreams. And I remember waking from the dream in a desperate fever. Dead phone lines. Unanswered letters. Lonely sheets. And bruised love thrown to its knees. The floor it's only brace. The snow drifting in as summer disappeared.

Girls, Girls, Girls

(a girl is a girl is a girl if she says she is)

A girl is a revolution
A girl is a cunt
A girl is a constitution
The definition
The composition
The de-evolution
A girl is the resolution
The action
The motion
The vision
A girl is your ignorance
A girl is her indignation
A girl is click bait
Fat ass
Skinny waist
Skinny waste
Wet thighs
A girl is a tongue
A girl is a reason
A riot
A girl is defiance
A girl is murder
A girl is the kill
A girl is predator
Is prey
The pretty thing
The dirty secret
A girl is silence
A girl is an outcry
A girl is in protest
A girl is a girl is a girl
A girl is a girl
A girl
A girl
A girl

i started using a menstrual cup and this cycle has been different

The first time I used a tampon I broke my hymen

The first time I had sex didn't hurt

Well, it hurt, but not inside
Well inside, but not my cervix

The cervix is the window to the heart

Or something

I'm saying that I said no, but we were young, and it was our first time, and I didn't know yet that no could mean no

We don't fuck anymore, but we're still friends, and once he told the room at large about how he likes to "skull-fuck his wife's mouth upside down"

Is she smiling or is that a frown?
Smile once for yes and frown upside down for no

The disgust I feel with my blood left some time in my teens, but body and blood aren't the same thing, just ask the savior

/not my savior, but you know the guy, the martyr, the one who knows a guy, the here, hold my beer guy that can do it all with no fear guy, the jack of all trades guy, the guy who plays guitar, totally respects women, but what's a g-spot? And what's the clit? And I like to skull-fuck my wife, but I'm a hopeless romantic, and would totally die for you, guy/

The disgust I feel for my body ebbs and flows and it's easiest to see low vs high tide by checking my hemline

There's something about a clump of tissue-soaked rags that screams dissociate
There's something about the way the crimson hits the basin, puddles across the surface-tension, spills and clots like watercolors that screams immersion

39

I would tamp down my depression, but

I'm just so much more of a snowflake millennial when I'm holding a blade
and a rope—

I'm pro-mood stabilizer, pro-anti-psychotic, pro-choice when I'm being PC,
pro-abortion when you can't wrap your head around it, pro-trauma
informed, pro-Black Lives Matter, pro-environmental preservation, pro-
pronouns, pro-gay rights, pro-trans & non-binary rights, pro-female rights,
pro-BIPOC rights, pro-human rights, pro-why the fuck do we even have to
say these things, pro free-healthcare, pro-non-denominational education, pro-
separation of church & state, pro-vaccinations, pro-paying creatives for their
work, Omggggg, yes, I called it their work, pro-defunding the police, pro-
therapy, pro-empathy, pro-sarcasm to get through the world collapsing
around us, and I'm making it a joke to make the poem work, but there's
more than one good reason why I wake up with ideations,

I named my son Atlas, and I regret it most days, because the past generations
just keep heaping their shit onto the next, and yeah, I wake up with fucking
cotton-mouth from the pills, but it stops the existential dread of knowing
you can't save anyone, yes, I usually cry after therapy, no, I don't want an
abortion, but yes, I think women should be allowed to own their own bodies,
yes, I understand that some of these issues don't affect me personally, but no,
I don't think that means that someone else should have to do all the fighting,
because yes, I think we should be amplifying voices, and no, I don't know
what weapons to bring to this fight, no, I don't think that the oxygen levels
will become uninhabitable before I die, only after, but yes, I'm all rubbed-
raw, anyway, because why the fuck do we even have to say these things, why
do we have to say these things, I am so fucking sick of saying these things,

And I'd love to set down my depression, but I can't when the only table is
our children's shoulders

a stigmata of the mouth

i think about icicles, ride the tracks to my mama, a teenager in the back seat, and a bump that lodged a needle-thin candy cane into the roof of her mouth, metallic saliva drips to the dirty underground, emerges in my toddler lap in the backseat with the roof of my own mouth bleeding from a scalpel-shaped hard candy, the hole hangs on through the years, i don't know the way to bandage the mouth, i pray that my injuries don't speed to meet my children's soft palates

Lambs

in third grade i learned that tiffany's mom and dad screamed like naked animals, but it didn't mean anything to me. all the parents were upset and said that tiffany was going to grow up to be a slut (*i mean come on, her name is tiffffaneeee, what were her parents thinking? and did you know she is friends with that jenna girl in fifth grade? but no, that's her brother's girlfriend, are you sure they are friends? maybe she didn't know about the sex, maybe her brother told her, maybe there is hope after all, but did you see how short her skirt is? and, her name is tiffany. i mean, really. anyway, isn't this the same girl that told the kids that she saw her santa presents in the closet before christmas? remember that mess? all i know is that they need to kick her off the cheerleading squad, those girls don't need that kind of reputation, imagine if the other schools knew that tiff taught the girls about fucking? don't call it fucking, that's not very christian*), so i asked my cousin about the naked animal screaming, and she drew me a picture of two people in a bed, with blankets carefully strewn over everything but the woman's breasts. i guessed this meant that tits were considered public even though naked screaming like animals was supposed to be private until you were a slut. after tiffany quit cheerleading, most girls wouldn't talk to her, so she hung out with a lot of guys, and "slut" still didn't really mean anything to me except for screaming like naked animals, which also didn't really mean anything to me. by the time animal screaming started, i had forgotten about the warning, and we were all sluts, anyway.

we probably would have dropped it, if we weren't required to pick up our rosaries and repent
hail mary, keep me clean. our father, why are girls sluts, when men watch for what lies behind our teeth?

when i was ten i was afraid to eat ice cream cones because something told me it would be too unholy to watch a young mouth suck at the tip, to tongue at the softness
breathing in the feminine tense makes this your responsibility, makes the compromise motherhood or sluthood, makes the threat the only option, whispers keep your mouth holy, keep your hands clean

forgive me, for i have sinned, my last confession was dripping with sticky sarcasm, and honestly i think it's pooling from between my legs into the baptismal fount, but that's only me trying to love my neighbor

I spend hours online reading about how many sexual assault victims use kink as a curative coping tendency to make sure I'm not more fucked up than I thought

I shy away from tight necklines that choke and constrict, keep them low and showy, because I prefer the weight of hands at my throat to the modesty of fabric on skin, and maybe I'm screaming to take me, or maybe I'm just screaming about how I shouldn't have to worry about being taken

Maybe my mind is your bedroom, I'm tanned-skin, freckled and bare, tied down against your mattress, maybe I'm bruised-flesh begging for my next spanking, pouting wet-eyed for blood, or it could just be that my mind is all these bedrooms, it could be night terrors, it could be I'm begging, I'm pouting, I'm wet-eyed for all the times I've been made to bleed

"Stop burning bridges
and drive off of them"

You buried me in the middle of a poem about me as the villain, but I forgive
you
Or I lied when I said I forgive you
Or I didn't lie because it felt like too much energy to not forgive you
I only have the energy to lie

If I'd had more energy, I would have told you about my lack of energy. I
would have told you how I woke up in bed and spent my days in bed and
then couldn't sleep in bed.

I wake in the middle of a meeting about reminding me to remember the
times I've felt abandoned, and that's the last thing I remember.

I crash into a letter about how I feel alone, and the other end of the phone
line tells me I'm too disconnected to be allowed to feel lonely, so I go back
to bed where I don't sleep because I only have the energy to lie.

I forgive you in the middle of a poem about me as the villain that only
remembers to forget how to lie.

Trigger Warning
for the Color in the Bath

Miss the cradle, miss the cradle, miss the cradle
But the water
I'm bruising porcelain, again
I feign infection
Drip sugar from both ends
But the water
I devour mud in fistfuls
There is a belief in returning home
There is a damnation in refilling the vessel
But the water
The water is in protest
And the water
And the water
And and and
And
I bow down to knees
Scrub the saturation from the grout
The clock is too heavy
Its arms always drag toward the ground
But the water
I collapse under leeching
White light as a spiral
And the water
The water scrapes behind walls of flesh
Exhausts the infrastructure
I shovel out celebrations
But the water
Confetti drops the beat too early
I watch the colors coalesce
But the water
A cherub spits itself out in my palm
But the water is the grave

16

remember the sunday-night strobe lights/remember flooding that basement
with resentment and regret/i punched you, and you threw me into a wall and
then threw the guy next to me for good measure/he hit the left edge of me,
and there was a body-sized hole in the drywall but no one seemed to care/i
saw it in flashes while they hit the lights over and again, but the floor was
slick, and by the time we got up off the ground it seemed inconsequential/i
sweat off my make-up and we passed out, beer-soaked in the bedroom on the
first floor/i woke up bruised and smiling/and sometimes i still wake up
bruised, smiling

but we don't hold hands anymore
we don't make eye contact anymore

because of that other time/remember that time/it was when i took advantage
of your aching and you took advantage of my loneliness/i read to you while
you watched tv/and there was no strobe light, but the blue had a bit of a
flicker/i passed out in my clothes, and you were still beer-soaked and
flooded with resentment, and i was still sweating out all my regrets/and you
played itsy-bitsy-spider up my left thigh/and your hand left a body-shaped
hole in my chest/no one really seemed to notice/and when i woke up three
days later and it was already easter sunday, it seemed inconsequential/and i
don't sleep smiling anymore/but sometimes i still wake up bruised

Ode to Mytyl

—After The Blue Bird (1940)

My poor girl,
Don't you know it's a trick?
Haven't you heard that once you give it up, they'll never return it?

But Mytyl,
It's that damned Berylune
With her fleeting magic
That Light is only an illusion
A gauzy distraction
See how she never steps down the path?

        Here's the problem, love
        It's always been your bluebird they wanted

Babe,
Why shouldn't we set the world on fire?
I've got a match in my back pocket
Tylette had it right
We should have ran
We should have whispered in the trees' ears
We should have burned the forest to scorched earth
Left those shining children in the clouds
Stop haunting ourselves with unfulfilled premonitions

Mytyl,
My poor girl,
You don't belong birthing their needs
You would have been better off in black & white
Forget the technicolor

Mytyl,
My love,
We should have snapped the bird's neck
Pinned the feathers in flight
Raised our dead at midnight
I'd build you a nest of broken bones
I'd let you dream your nights in shades of blue

> Just me and you
> And on our mantle, your bluebird
> too

Protest Sounds

I was a battle cry. I was the shouting of many throats and the raising of many fists. I was feet treading concrete. And I was running on energy-spent. I was fuel-level low. I was the pilot asleep in the cockpit. And I have been reborn as the plane-crash. A lost fight. My script warped into three ceding letters, DNR. This is what democracy looks like when it resigns. Buckles. Succumbs. Submits. But it's not so much a white flag. It's more like they told me that humble pie tasted of sleep, and I was fucking exhausted. And I would have swallowed the fucking moon for a chance at peace. But I woke as the plane-crash. And I know that sounds like the phrase giving up, but really the plane still explodes. The gasoline still burns. The fuselage will ignite when enough pressure is applied. Rattle my cage. I dare you. I am burying ghosts tonight in the hopes of bringing them back to life. Midnight resuscitation. Voice, cocked and loaded with bullets shaped like a resurrection spell. Me as the voice I lost along the way. I am drawing chalk outlines of what an activist looks like stuck in neutral, so that I can erase them with a jumper cable to the heart. Tick, tock, tick, tock, tick, tock, boom. Remember me as the echo in the night. Remember me as impassioned. Remember me as ready to burn it all down. And when weeds grow through the ash, know that is me relearning to spread. That is myself as a wild fire. That is myself, conquering my own sleeping self.

what happens when the girl erupts?

i. a girl is a dead thing

  a. not yet buried

  b. born dead

ii. a girl is the place where it hurts

  a. do you know the place where it hurts

    I. you sleep with the lights on and wake with them off/there is too much bright for all of this dark/there is not enough bright to fend off all of this dark

    2. an injury that ruptures blood vessels under the skin is called a bruise/a girl is thin-skin, stretched over violent capillaries/contusion, hematoma, bleeding-tissue/these all make up a girl/a girl can take a beating/thin-skin cannot always take a beating/you should tally platelets/you should prepare a girl for bruising

iii. a girl is thin-skinned

  a. a girl is a ghost

  b. a girl is a disappearing act

    I. the ghost and the disappearing are ultimately the same thing/a girl cannot hold her own shape/a girl cannot be there when she needs to be/cannot leave when she needs to leave/you can call this drifting/thin-skin avoids the blades/thin-skin has been known to beg for the blade

  c. the transparency is the thing of note

    I. you can eat a secret/dab at your mouth/suck the whisper from between your teeth/you should not flaunt the way a girl is a secret/the way a girl is too full

    2. there are reasons why this skin is always stretched to capacity

    3. a girl can only hold so much

iv. a girl is a vessel

  a. a girl can only hold so much

v. what happens when the girl is filled

my teeth have teeth of their own

—After Shriya Bajpai

Velvet's crushed in gold
The seeds burst life
Chalk outline the direction

They expect the dead
They expect lifeless

There is always the prodding
Always the pinning
The pining
The pawing, pecking, prying

               Never the permission

They all claim stability
See, how they believe themselves statuesque
Now I laugh through the crumbling

I do not need you
I do not need the prodding, pinning, pining, the pawing, pecking, prying

I melt the honey between their bones
Caress the soft belly, supplicant
Let them kiss dirt

I never wanted to eat from cupped palm

It was only a titter
A flirting
A flutter
A simper

I reach hands down throat, pull skeletons through limp skin, watch the hollows crawl

They all call me snake charmer because of the way the slithering up my skirts stops
never-
The-less I'd rather make a clean cut at the head than settle into the enchantment

I've never feigned kitten
This is lion's den

Whisper,
See how we're different,
You could never sleep here

I would never
Let you
sleep here

Kinks

Something about the place on the shower wall where your hair sticks. Stomach spins. I've heard some people /like/ to play with wet hair. Nausea. Confusion. Disgust.

And I remember once, I stayed in your dorm room. And she stayed too. And I slept on the couch. Fucking (fuck-ing) roommate cum stains. Or spilt salt-water? Unsure. But, here's to hoping. And when I say slept. What I mean is. I stayed at your dorm. But she stayed. And I covered my face with some dirty, dingy pillow. And soft, green/blue/maybe orange? bullshit, half-dead, alley-way light poured in from inner-city, barred, second-floor windows. But I didn't sleep. Because she stayed. So instead. I listened to the fucking boat rock on the fuck-stain, threadbare couch. And every now and then she'd breathe hard. And the knocking would stop. And then laughter. And oh, by the way. Did I mention your roommate burnt soup a few hours before. And some perv with a crush slept on the floor next to my worn-down, plush grave of bodily fluids. Black-light sensitive. The whole fucking (fuck-ing) room. And perv laid, eyes wide open, hand down pants. And she panted. And the bed/boat knocked/rocked. And we both listened. Me, ceiling staring. Him, bug-eyed, me staring. And I wish there was a goddamn fan in that room. And I wish there wasn't her hair on the shower wall.

double helix

blame it on the ghosts
blame it on the rain
blame it on the placement of stars in correlation with planets
blame it on the gunshots
the poverty line
the humanity
the lack of humanity
blame the lack of sleep
blame the mother
blame the father
mostly blame the results

here's the problem, i was never touched enough or maybe i was touched
enough but it just wasn't the right kind of touch or maybe i was touched too
much and now nothing is enough or maybe none of those is the problem but
there is definitely a problem

/here's the problem/

my heart is the largest muscle in my body
but that's not my only problem
my light is the smallest muscle in my body
my heart can only hold back so much dark

/here's the problem, i'm blaming the problem, again/

there are things that run in the veins, and my light started pumping mud
before i was born or maybe i was born in the mud or the mud was born from
my light or the light was born covered in mud

we can blame it on the afterbirth even if it came beforebirth

we can blame it on the ghosts

ghosts come before and after
ghosts can come before and after birth

Barefoot Desperados

When I was 17, I used to hang out at this collective called the BAC House. It was probably one of the most interesting points in my life. It was in the slums, so we got away with a lot of chaos for a long time. They would do folk-punk shows there every night. A lot of the time no one would even have instruments. I once saw someone add to the rhythm section by sweeping the ground with a broom aggressively. "I'm doin' the sweepin'." It was pots and pans bands. On Saturday nights they'd host panty parties. We'd all mosh and skank in our underwear outside or in the basement. I'd leave covered in sweat and sneak into a private beach where I'd pass out until I knew my dad was in bed. There were four bedrooms and 26 people living there, most of them barely older than me. Not to mention the people like me who would pop in whenever they felt like they needed a safe place. Sometimes there was food. Sometimes not. The backyard was fenced in, but there was a cliché fence board that could swing out so the residents could sneak into the neighbor's yard and steal food off the grill. Most of the time the water was turned off and we would run the neighbor's garden hose to a kiddie pool in the backyard. The cops were called all of the time. We were loud. We were wild. There were too many people coming and going. At one point during the summer there were two dogs, a squirrel, and 18 cats living in the house. Plus chickens outside. The bathroom and kitchen were constantly covered in feathers and fur and with the lack of running water, every surface was filthy. I didn't eat there even when there was food. I never wore shoes then, and there were animal droppings everywhere. I caught E Coli that summer, and it made sex painful. It could have been the hose water. Or the carpet of shit in the bathroom. I doubt it. That summer was the first time I was raped. And it could have been the rape. It never stopped after that. I spent more time in the safe haven these kids had created, avoiding the rest of my life. Towards the last days of summer, the cops were being called on us every day. The landlord finally said *no more* when some of the guys staged a protest in front of the house to "riot for the right to noise." They had a week to evacuate. I was there the day they broke all the windows.

We spray painted every wall. Three bands played in the living room, simultaneously, and we moshed through every room. We threw each other into walls in order to raze them. People were crowd surfing to get a better angle to punch the ceilings out. Three girls swung from the ceiling fan to pull it down to the floor. We lit fireworks in the kitchen and bedrooms and fireplace. They set the animals free. They took lighters and spray paint to scorch the old, plaster walls and wooden floors. Someone posted grainy photos on MySpace. I didn't have a profile, and I couldn't see the screen, but I heard ukulele storytelling, describing each scene in detail. And when everyone was worn out and had released their wild, we climbed on the roof to watch the sun set. Some of the guys took turns jumping from the roof to the kiddie pool. They probably got hurt, but at seventeen and twenty, ankles bounce back. We threw the rest of the fireworks from the roof, already lit. They'd explode too close to the ground, and some of them caught in the grass. I left early and slept on the beach. The police came that night and everyone who was left was held overnight. They never got the deposit back on the house. I haven't had E Coli since we broke up.

Dissonance in Discord

It's the disconnect
The taut-skin stretch
The scabbed-knee split
We pay for the ache
For the want
The inflection is placed where the need arises
I choke down white light then spill out dark, I can't keep preying on the
resonance, this is not lyrical, this is predator in the grass, sleight of hand
I'm saying I still hear drips in the attic
Drips in the basement
Drips in my head
It's in your head in your head in your head
I'm saying the repetition is a flood
A storm
A lesson in the act of drowning
And as a reminder
I don't know how to swim
As a reminder
I still hold my breath
As a reminder
I've stopped holding on, I'm arched-back, given-in, I take on water, sink into
lacking, into forgotten format
We pay for the pleasure of repeating ourselves
For the ways we prey on the act of repeating ourselves
This is only compulsory
Only in your head
There's a paranoia in the repetition
It's in your head in your head in your head

ECHO(echo)

how many years do you get to hold me/
against the floor of your bedroom?

/my bones were

not built for this/

i keep thinking i
can ascend to heaven and
when they move the
boulder from the tomb,
you'll have descended to
hell, and this will be my
resurrection.

deliver us from
thought/deliver us from
reality.

but i still wake
up three days later with the
same wounds that i fell
asleep with. this is not
stigmata.

ECHO - you

how long will i wake up with my knees bruised from the fall?

ECHO – didn't

and no, not that fall. there were no wings.
i've never been angelic.

ECHO - ask

but 3 feet from the bed to the floor leaves its own damage, and i can't seem
to heal.

i keep trying to
drown myself in the bath.
force these small deaths
from my chest. swallow
something clean because
everything inside has your
fingerprints. i keep trying

to brush away the spots
where you linger, but
there's bruising here. there's
bruising here, and i'm
willing to bet you didn't
realize how much you can
fit inside of a bruise. i'm
betting you don't know
what hangs around under
the skin after you leave.
there's pent up aggression
here.

we can dissect this/this is what nephrotic looks like.

scalpel, please?

ECHO – you

didn't ask

if you cut here,
you'll see where your hands
catch between my thighs.
your fingers will come
across a drought, but you're
hungry not thirsty, and you
were raised to swallow a
meal without drink. slice
deeper for the moment
when i realize, no won't
mean no this time. that
word drips around us,
viscous, tangible. remove
that tissue on the right.
there's an open window
pouring snow. and i always
thought the white light was
a myth, but i must admit
that i am blinded. there's
new year's day dangling in
the air and new year's eve
still clinging to your breath.
and there's bleeding now,

but we can staunch that.
there's screaming, but
distress is easily muted.
arms, meet blanket. lungs,
meet hand at throat.
mouth, meet floor. back,
meet knees.

there's too much
movement, and none of it
is mine. i'm on my face. i'm
kissing the hardwoods,
shaded crimson and oak. i
am the way my bones dig
into the ground. i am the
way my wrists will stain
indigo and violet for days. i
am the vomit that comes
after. i am the sweat you
kiss from my forehead. i
am the fever post-
ascension. was that as holy
for you as it was for me?

and i don't have
to explain the ECHO at
this point.

i didn't ask for this. (echo)

i am shirt pulled up around my wrists, twisted in stronger hand.

i am face wet, silent.

i am no/no/no/no/no please, not today. and i am the negative until it's a
double, and did i negate this somehow? and maybe two wrongs make a right?
but this isn't adding up.

i didn't ask for this. (echo)

but this is no resurrection.

I didn't ask for this. (echo)

hark, the darkness sings.

No Inheritance

I found another lump today more precisely found two the discomfort lies in
the reality that they are no longer congregating in the same area the body is a
temple and these passengers are worshiping separate gods the thing about
gods is I found two lumps today and I know the way a temple can be a curse
I know there is no sacred ground no matter how often the roses push
through

This body was grown not given
Grown not given
Grown not given
Grown not given

Weeds

I'm going to hit him. And he'll fucking hit me back. Because that's what he does. He fucking hits me. But his mouth just keeps running. And my fingers tap. And my wrists itch. And my jaw sits tense and tight. Clenched like his fists at the end of the night. And the truth is, I won't ever hit him. I'll come in sharp with the words. Cut the tension of his fucking, bullshit monologue. And as the cord snaps back, the recoil will be his hands at my throat. And he'll squeeze too hard. Like the too-quick palm closing over lightning bugs in summer. And he'll toss me room to room. Dandelion seeds breaking away from the over-zealous tug. And I'll plant blood across the threadbare, stained carpet. And they'll bloom next spring as puckered scars across my toes. They'll flourish, broken blood vessels below my eyes, careening across my cheek bones. And they'll wither in the cold when the electric in my veins is out. When there's no one home to pay the bills. As the heat leaves me in floods. And I'll have to carry this baggage beneath my eyes because I fear the weight of sleep. And I'm unsure where else I can keep it. Because I've only ever owned broken bones and tired eyes. I've only ever owned a bloodied nose and spent muscles. So, I'll gnaw at these roots that ensnare me at the ankles. I'll rip myself from the flesh of this space. And my mind will sleep somewhere else tonight, while my body waits for the next gust of wind to come and plant me back across the floor of this broken home.

And I won't ever fucking hit him.

Evanescent

The wings are   beating   a dead horse, again
I watch a welt rise   from the grave between each finger-length of
skin, and I know you never imagined me graceful
But that's only a thought now   a cyclone in the memory,
     not an iceberg in reality's ocean

What does Seven know of holiness, after all?

Seven knows a pew-bench straining the back, Seven knows the cheek cradles
the phone into a wound, Seven knows the floor isn't   clean
enough to eat off of

I pick a hair from between teeth, remove the tissue from the eyes, pray to the
carpet

Seven knows the hymn for an apology is a late-night courtesy call   a
closed
     door tantrum
Seven falls from a mountain-top and lands on   Six

Six blows a dandelion wish into a lilac, cries a strobe light, holds a bullet in
its palm
Six offers you a halo, wonders that they ever thought themselves
     hallowed, wonders at the necessity of worship, worship,
     warship

Seven comes to
Seven steals the bullet, places it in the thigh   suffers the injury
on behalf of Six
Seven can take the sting
Seven says   fire-away

Seven becomes sacrosanct   though earth-bound
     becomes its own sacrifice

Where It Hurts

Your hands are often too rough. The skin at the edges of your nail beds is peeled back and hardened and has, on occasion, been known to bleed without warning. If I run my thumb along the inside of your palm, I know exactly where it will catch on raised callouses. And even when I'm alone, I can feel the spot where your fingers would rest in the webbing of my own. My skin is electric shocks at the thought of the places where your fingertips most often linger. Nerve endings, attention-wrought. Breath, hitched in tightrope suspension. And I can count your freckles without you in the room. I could draw a map of your skeleton from memory. Place each rib in its exact location. Carve the precise depth of your clavicle. I know the pattern your teeth leave on each of my hips and how your tongue feels restless against my own. My neck can recall each spot where your lips chap and how often your front teeth push past them. I am violently aware of the spots where your hair refuses to lie against your scalp and instead reaches skyward. The sighs and stutters that litter your speech patterns. I can feel the sharp intake of your breath when my teeth close just a bit too hard on your frame. And that slight leak of CO_2 in nighttime stillness. I sleep, dizzy in your exhales as they fill up my inhales. I would swear I have been constructed from the realization of the space that you fill in relation to all of the emptiness I leave behind. And you forgot the color of my eyes.

12.10.22

There's a reminder that this will always burn too deep
Wrap around my fourth finger, second from the left finger
I'm saying you played me for keeps and that sounds romantic when the reader misses
the part where the ring is actually wrought around my neck
The reader misses the part with the soldering iron pressed against the umbilical cord
You miss the part when I say no, so I miss the part where I lay open-leg splayed and
you teach my body how to melt skin to skin
I'm not saying I blame my rape for subsequent abuse, but that's only because I'm not
saying
I'm not saying that I blame you when I look into my son's eyes and see my terror
reflected back
I'm not saying I blame your forced double helix for my uncertainty that I'll pluck it
from his bloodstream and make something more innocent, more stable, more me than
you
I'm saying you're a taker and you took and I'm saying you fucked me in more ways
than one and you fucked me after I said no and you fucked me up and you fucked me
into the fucking future
Because I'm saying I don't know how to trust and so I give it away freely to anyone
who shows up and I keep making violent choices because when you asked to give me
violence I declined and you forced me into violence and I'm saying that I'm not
blaming my rape but that's only because I'm not saying that the reader always misses
the part where you rape me

4.2.22

I woke with yesterday's thoughts strung up between my bones

1. I am the problem—paranoid

    a. I poisoned the tides, the fish are all dead-eyed, belly up, the water is crashing into reality, churning into an acid-bath, no one becomes a superhero, we both die in the end

    b. I should have made something sweet, melted flesh down, whipped myself into sun-spun sugar, smoothed my throat into bird-song, caramelized my lungs, ground my breasts into honey, cardamom-covered collarbones, bones for flour, scones for dinner

    c. I know how to sew, I run my lips through the machine guard, straight-edge, neat-stitched, I won't make a sound

    2. I am the problem—no need to continue

Call It a Resolution

We don't exchange gifts anymore,
You hold me down on New Year's Eve,
My teeth hit the hardwoods,
My "no" comes out bloody—
I pretend I see mistletoe.

Ouroboros

Tell me why at this age I still have to convince myself that not everyone need
be forgiven
Some mornings I still wake up choking on the excuses I made for you

Some mornings

/my skirt was too short/my laugh was leading/my voice was too soft/too
little/too much/too/

I was raised to teach and I am too used to teaching my shooter how to shoot
Too used to handing you over the loaded gun
Too used to unbuckling my armor to welcome the shot
I was born wrapped in a white flag, and it took me too long to realize I was
allowed to shed that skin

But some mornings, I remember

/dragons will eat their own tails/I cut my losses/devour the mistake/

Lima Echo Tango/Mike Echo/Golf Oscar

I printed the paperwork on pastel because I ran out of white, spent the next week worrying that the courts would deny a signature on pink or a birthdate on green. The real threat was the way that the dissolution was always in your hands. You've never given for nothing. Taker, taker, taking, always taking, taking. I run a finger against your brow, wipe the hangover from your mouth. Please, let me go. You never signed off. I flashback to static airlines and whistling gunfire calling from the Middle East. Whisper, please, please, let me go. You perfected your disappearing act while my body perfected the act of swelling. 36 weeks in, and I birthed the consequence of falling in love with a missing person's report. I never got the chance to call the reward number. I know the way it's not worth calling. Please, let me go. I know the prize. I know the bruised hipbones. I know the raw-flesh-tongue, post-bite. I know the stretching belly. The lower abdomen scarring. The hormone flood. Please, let me go. Let me go. Let me go. And you're taking. And I know the way it's not worth calling. I know it's not worth calling.

I pray for an empty bed.

Birth as a Trauma

my daughter holds me under water, and I wonder whose fists these are, choke me like you mean it, I ache in the pit, burnt through like the after-math, holding still is not an option, the thrashing is born on the waves of thrashing, is this the way the cradled waist becomes the strangled throat, is this the acid reaching from inside, is this the discomfort of living inside myself, I want out too, I want to be the exit, wet drips between legs, the water crimsons, I want in shades of scarlet

4

The point is transparency, and I've been opaque for too long
The tip of the needle is hollow
We stick in the base of the knot
There is impossibility buried in the thickness
July holds me down and ties confusion around my wrists
You claim your rape as more traumatizing than my own and I wonder when
you stopped supporting other victims
I wonder if you stopped supporting victims or stopped supporting me
Uncertainty follows me across the country
I bury my head in the mattress
I could suffocate on your absence

You're Not Always the You of the Poem

And you don't want to, but you know how to fake a smile

And it's not really fair, but you're living like you were born on the edge of a
laugh line, like you'll go out with a simper, with a giggle, not with a bang

And you're the only one who knows how your birth was a cradle shaped like
a coffin, how the weight at your neck keeps pushing you to the grave

And you lose days to sadness
And you lose days to acting
And you lose days forcing the corners of your mouth up

And inside
And inside, a cacophony
And inside, hoarse throat floats a noise across your tongue
And outside
And outside, the wings are thrumming
And outside, a smile

And still you know the voice with which the broken bird sings

The Year is 2021
—*After Kait Quinn*

I am the dreamer
The year is 2021
I lie in bed
I am unsure if my eyes are open or closed

There is a way that darkness plays tricks. Calls itself mischief. Calls itself
seen, throughout the absence of seeing. I am under blankets with a hand
pressed to my back. There is the hand pressed to my back and the hand over
my mouth. I eat my own screams from the palm.

I am the dreamer
The year is 2021
I lie in bed
I am unsure if my eyes are open or closed

My eyes are open. I hide in the room without a window. I hide under worn
quilt. Under inked-skin and borrowed clothes. My eyes are open. The smoke
curls beneath me. The body curls beneath me. The promises are open-ended.
The promises are lost.

I am the dreamer
The year is 2021
I lie in bed
I am unsure if my eyes are open or closed

My eyes are closed. The monitor shrieks. The space between raw throats is
equal to the time that is left. The time closes. The throat closes. My eyes are
closed. I shriek for a reckoning. I shriek through raw throat. The time lies
behind closed-doors. The time is lost.

I am the dreamer
The year is 2021
I lie in bed
I am unsure if my eyes are open or closed

There is a way the darkness screams from the palm. Screams open-ended screams. Screams behind closed-doors. I am dreaming behind eyes unsure if they are open or closed. I promise with both eyes open. I shriek with both eyes closed. There is a way they are open. There is a way they are closed.

I am the dreamer
The year is 2021
I lie in bed
I am unsure if my eyes are open or closed

I am the palm
I am eyes open
I am eyes closed
I am the darkness
See how I open
See how I'm closed

I am the dreamer
The year is 2021
I lie in bed
My eyes do not open or close

Please Take Your Ghost from My Son

It's October, and I'm thinking about how you haven't seen your son in five years. I'm thinking of how his eyes and his mouth are both the shape of mine, but how the way he holds them is nothing like the way I hold my own. I'm thinking of heavy shadows behind his 9-year-old eyes. Of the freckles that dust his nose that clearly do not belong to me. I'm traveling backwards. And it's October. And I'm thinking of your hand on my swollen belly. I'm thinking of how I wasn't ready. I wasn't ready. I wasn't ready. And, I wasn't ready. But there's your hand over my mouth, so the words sound muffled. Your hand on the back of my neck. Your hand too strong. And how I always blame everyone and everything but you. It wasn't your fault. It was Corporal Hayden's fault for getting shot in front of you and not being able to stop himself from bleeding out. It was your mom's fault for being raped in front of you. It was the alcohol's fault. Or it was my fault. It was the truck you totaled. It was the way my wedding band always sat too loose and how it was so easy to throw back at you. It was Jeffrey's fault for waking you up screaming all of those nights. Or maybe it was your dad's fault for making you think that strong hands counted for something more than skin and bones and tears. It's October and I'm thinking of how my body felt betrayed as it expanded to fit the shape of something that I never asked for. It's October and I'm thinking of how that shape has your hairline and something behind his eyes. It's October and I'm finally blaming you for all the things that you stole

CamBaby···

you want to watch me suck my boyfriend's dick

Profile reads: DM for custom requests! Currently have premade deep mouth/throat, giantess, foot, menstruation, plug, masturbation, & toy content, but open to other customs as well <3

The XXX tiers include all of my solo content for free!

Private message caveat reads: absolutely no scat play, no cum, urine, shit, vomit, or other bodily fluids on my face or in my hair, does not do piggy, I do not have an endoscope and will not film lower than vocals, do not ask or you will be restricted from private messaging. I do not squirt.

Freshman year I was sexually assaulted in a maintenance closet between AP English and Bio class. He kept his hand over my mouth and licked my neck. There was no penetration, but there were fingers circling my clit and a hard cock pressing at the small of my back.

I wouldn't kiss anyone for the next 10 months.

Sophomore baby, in tight shirts, tight pants, with black bandana, violet hair, headphones ever-present, falls in love for the first time, we strip down to under clothes and dance in a summer storm, roll against crumpled sheets, ache and ache and ache for the kind of infinity you can only believe in at 16, until

Until I'm a head pressed down over a rising mound in his pants, until I'm gagging and weeping out betrayal, until I'm realizing we were never infinite, we were new-born, fledgling, unsure how to navigate desires, broken-winged, begging the other to do the mending

You're, "babe, I saw your heart shaped uvula and I came so fucking hard when you moaned, how does $50 to watch you suck your man sound?"

I'm playing baby, again, I'm all pouty lips, breathy voice, hair twirled around index finger, agreement,

Until

Until you're pushing boundaries, you're, "I want him to cum on your face or I am not paying for this shit, what am I supposed to do with this? At least he could have slapped you with his cock!"

And I'm airy,
"Aw daddy, I don't do degradation kinks, it says in the PM intro :("

But you still think that I have to do this. I don't have to be your sex, your hot drippy slut, your come here baby and fuck me harder, your please daddy spank me, I don't have to slurp your cum, and play kitten with limp wrist paws. This is pure choice. This is cat-scratch fever and I want to spread it.

I'm a growling little mistress, and you're paying plus 10 for unclear instructions

I purr, gentle. Fuck myself to sleep.

3.30.22

The pavement cracks a little deeper with each winter, and my knees are a splintered mirror, a filly falls and falls, the film loops, the crumbling grows to standing, the standing eats the filly, becomes the mare, I become tender muscle, tense sinew,

This morning I coughed up a cadaver, palm size, a miniature death, I stained the tiles the color of a poltergeist, the pavement cracks, the grout splits,

The mare is sticky between the legs, blackberry compote clumping at her feet, the pit of the fruit blinks in slow motion, her knees hit concrete, she becomes a backwards aging, I help her pick the eyelashes from the syrup, we weep in unison

O, sleepy seasons!
—After Charles Baudelaire

Cold fingers, small boned, thin skinned
The bird flies from knuckles
Every day is winter bound
A knot in the back, cracked spine
The seeds are birthing shadows
I bend at the waist, but not the right way
Petechiae sprawls like constellations across cheekbones
I dream it's a blush
It will end in the night
The sleeping is never enough
O, the sleeping is never enough!

I learned today that Bridget Jones was trying to lose 20lbs because she weighed 135

I fell in love with a skeleton smile when I learned my midriff would show in my new cheer uniform, you show off your waist once, and the world never lets you go back into hiding.

There is always the comparison

Say this many less

This many less

This many less

This many less

Please. Please, say less, less, less

My navel was a part of my mother and my navel causes me trauma

My mother's navel has also caused her trauma

And my mother's mother

My grandma's navel was a part of many other navels before it was traumatic

My grandma can only eat certain foods

My grandma stayed in hospitals

My grandma destroyed a few organs

My grandma almost disappeared

My grandma says don't let your navel cause trauma

And my navel still likes to cause me trauma, because once you show your waist, the world never lets you go back into hiding.

I try to kiss the plate, but my navel isn't mine, and it's stuck in a time loop betraying us all, and I think how the only time I ever really prayed was before I put on my uniform or after I ate, and how those weren't the same types of praying, and how neither of those ended in belief

I think, less, less, please

Less.

Dear Lucy

Dear Lucy, stop sharing this way. You keep overloading the packages, and they break before they've arrived. Dear Lucy, I'm not trying to tell you what to do, I'm just trying to help, and yes, I know, you've heard that before. It's just that, I don't think that everyone gets where you're coming from. I don't think that everyone gets where they're coming from. Dear Lucy, I'm sorry that things happened this way. I'm sorry about how many things you can remember. And no. I don't think that most people have so many things to remember. And no. I don't know how to stop the memories, but Dear Lucy, it just runs in your family, this heaviness, and this running, Dear Lucy, I don't know what you mean about feeling too small and too large all at once, but I'm sure that you could just call it antithesis, Dear Lucy, Dear Lucy, have you tried sleeping? Have you been eating? Dear Lucy, you have to sleep, Dear, Lucy, stop crying, stop holding those hands, stop overfilling, you're not under-filled, and I swear one day you'll be full, if you'd just stop giving so much away, Dear Lucy, I think I understand now, and Dear Lucy, we're spiraling. Dear Lucy, don't leave. Dear Lucy, I'm leaving, stop writing me here.

but the moth sheds the caterpillar's fangs

And at once I remember why I sharpen teeth to points

I run the blade against the porcelain and forget the idea of wrapping myself in chrysalis rebirth as the spider spins excuses for why they should remain the same

silk /silk/ n.) a fine, strong, soft, lustrous fibre produced by silkworms in making cocoons and collected to make thread and fabric, also spun by some insect larvae and by most spiders

see also - soft /sôft/ adj.) having a pleasing quality involving a subtle effect or contrast rather than sharp definition

see also the way the delicate takes on the work, the way the soft, the way the silk is left with the effort

I sharpen teeth to points
I lose them post-cocoon

I promise there's a good reason why I refused for so long to release silk-soft wings

Snuff

You said you like it when I'm nervous. You said I'm cute with my hands covering my laugh and my fingers twirling my hair. You said you feel less awkward when I glance awkwardly into my own lap. You loved that aching squirm that helped you cover your own insecurities. You hated when you'd inhale a line and I'd sit calm and patient. Indifferent to your flaws. You liked to offer me drinks in front of everyone, knowing full well I'd say no. Knowing full well that everyone would keep offering all night. You liked to make me walk in front of you, stumbling over my steps the way I stumble over the words that fall from me into you. You didn't want to lead the way, afraid you might be the one to trip. You'd leave me at parties to see how long I'd wait. And lay claim to me in front of large groups so you could tell me later how you didn't mean it. And the worst would come when my discomfort would leave you vulnerable. I'd spend all night vomiting up delicate caterpillars. And you would take fists and boots to snuff out their prickly lives. And through power hungry fits, you'd confess your secrets late into the night. And as I devoured them, feeding myself into butterflies, your thoughts would become poisoned bile at the realization. And you would beg for me to hand over my safe-haven cocoons. Terrified that I may be more comfortable than you. Terrified that I may be growing while you sat in front of me with your guts on display. So you spin your spider web across my body, wrapped in carefully-crafted blankets of silk. And when I emerged, you burst forth from eggs and laid waste to my thriving. Because you like it when I'm nervous.

Girls in white dresses

I place our burgundy on Sunday clothes
It's the holy thing to do
I pray you'll check my marriage bed
Oh, my god, deliver us
Confirmation that
I'm suicidal again
Ave, Ave, Ave a bloody slut at the stake
Ave, Ave, Ave a girl who knows how to have a good time
A girl who can whisper to snakes
I want to be dirty-kneed on the chapel walls
I want to be crucified in stained glass
Tower saintlike in my persecution
Drip sticky-white across marble halls
I'll baptize the wedding bells
Rebirth them a funeral knell
Watch me split open
Leak out devil spell
Deliver me all spent and used to the churchyard
Into arms of men
Into beds of men
From gods
Deliver us
From men
Deliver us

I'll burn my own funeral pyre

—*After Brody Dalle*

They've learned how to rape us without lifting a cock, and I'm afraid of what will happen if we keep allowing them to use gasoline to reduce the friction

Here's a proposal—

We steal a match in preparation
We wait for the breaking
Wait for the entering
We're all kittens
All downward dogs, downward bitches being taken
It's mid-thrust when we strike

I go up like a torch in the night

We set the world on fire, but not the way they wanted

We press our hands around their throats
Bring mouths to their flaming ears

Whisper

I want you to crown me, right here on my knees

A Poem in Which I Talk to Myself Just Like in All of the Others

You watch the clouds roll off the backs of trees, and a bird slips from the sky

You give this monologue under water, nimble fingers pick at the knots, never unstring the rope of the net

The sun is an interlude, a slice in the pressure.
You think knife to tension.
You think mirrored pane against humidity.
You think heatstroke behind eyelids.

Hard stops deserve proper punctuation.

Forget the clawing at the neck and the way the feathers look plucked from the pale, forget the nest nestled safely above the scene, forget the contents, the bleating, the begging, the lungs, the outcry, forget the way you're needed, forget that you are the falling thing, you are the falling thing, forget to swim

A bird slips from the sky

you drop to your knees and we both pretend to know something about prayer

call me idol not god
call me righteous
waiting
vengeful
yesterday i realized you never dug inside me
surface wounds for surface tension
you never licked up the mess
a chalice is worth more than the meal
i place the flesh at your tongue, and you vomit in my direction
you were begging to be swallowed, but i ripped you open and fingered your
bleeding hollowness instead
there is no worship here
you're knee-bound from lack of fight, but the deal was euphoria
you may as well drop entrails between my thighs, something less than elastic,
less than statuesque
i'm all black lace, dainty, sunshine-rosebuds lining the cups
i spread my legs and hope you remember that i only ever wanted to save you
from grace

subdivisions

I found humanity the day my mother pushed me, bleeding, from between her legs. The retribution for that is the breath in my chest and the ability to see that people are not good to each other. The lines in the sand are faint with all of the times that they have been toed. I assure you the grass is not greener on this side. There is only more sand. Please stop craning your neck to spit over the privacy fence. The day that your mother pushed you bleeding from wherever you came is the day that you were given humanity. And that oxygen-weight filling your lungs makes you entitled to it. But does your neighbor not breathe as well? Each time the heart pumps blood through your veins you are given the right to birth opinions. And each time you push them, bleeding, from your mouth, you become the mother of your words. But please, keep your children on your side of the fence. And if some of them look like me, well I have mirrors over here, so you can keep those as well.

Roxanne
—After The Police

i. you don't have to wrap his tongue around your teeth and take the blame for his bleeding, avoid his tongue in fear of his bleeding, you don't have to, worry at his bleeding, at his tongue, worry at its squirming, gentle yourself, avoid scarring a fragile ego with your magnificent fangs, you don't have to,

ii. you don't have to, you don't have to taste like peaches, make yourself a sun-baked pie, sever yourself, slice yourself, break yourself into manageable, into bite-size, into swallow-me-whole, you don't have to be palatable, you never promised to temper your tart, you don't have to flush and blush, be sticky-sweet, sugar-spun, syrupy-slick,

iii. become an empty hole shaped like a warm mattress and supple arms, you don't have to, you don't have to, you don't have to stay the night, but you don't have to close your legs, lock the door, you don't have to

iv. you don't have to smell like jasmine and amber, you don't have to cover your sweat, wipe your brow, fear the fetid stains of your labor, you don't have to roll in the meadow or the garden or the forest, weave your hair with flower-crowns and lay prostrate for the bees, allow them entrance, pray they suckle at your teat, present the pollen as an offering,

v. you don't have to be the sacrifice for him, lay down your weapons and let him take credit for your fight, deliver your skin to his altar, you don't have to, you don't have to, you don't have to,

89

vi. salivate at everything that's harder than yourself, drool at how he thinks he's a wolf at a dog fight, a sword at a knife fight, you don't have to be impressed,

vii. you don't have to drown yourself in ink stains, you don't have to only whisper on paper, you don't have to silence your screams, or cover your mouth, or bite down on the headboard, the gag, the palm, the anthrax-soaked end of the protest, fill pockets with stones, bake your head at 350°, you don't have to,

viii. sharpen your spear, but if you want to stab, to end them all in a blood bath, you don't have to dull it either, because you don't have to

ix. resolve the conflicts, who said you were the mediator, the mother, the manager, the problem-solver, the peaceful one, you don't have to be, you don't have to,

x. you don't have to haunt your own nights, spend your insomnia-fevers stuck in your head, relive your days, forget to take the future by the throat, you don't have to take hardened hands to memories and pound them into dust, you don't have to take gentle hands to memories, apologize to your past like you're still only your past, you don't have to float over the bed, incite nightmares, tear your insides apart for dissection, linger over the healing wounds, you don't have to, you don't have to, you don't have to

4.10.22 or Frida

Weaponize me
Make me a Rorschach revolution
I want to spring forth from labor channel with the fight on the tip of my
tongue
Tumble from the cunt under gunfire and stick the landing

The problem with a girl born wrapped in roses is that the umbilical cord has
thorns

We could prune the flowers from my hair, but I want the overgrowth

I want the deadheads firing pollen bombs at the glass ceiling, I want the guts
pooling at my feet, I want the slime, the rot, the stink of it, I want to fuel the
ache,

I want to be birthed full-bloom,

I will caress the delivery,
Paint the blood across my brow

I want to sleep in the belly of the war,
I want to name myself

Notes on Previous Publication

"False Advertising" appeared in the *Divine Feminist Anthology* from Get Fresh Publishing & Issue 4 of *Her Words* from *Black Mountain Press*

"Lambs" also appeared in Issue 4 of *Her Words* from *Black Mountain Press* as well as *Issue VI – Li Ji: courage & the serpent* from *Free Verse Revolution*

"4.10.22 or Frida" also appeared in *Issue VI – Li Ji: courage & the serpent* from *Free Verse Revolution*

"THE MATCH THAT SET THE HOUSE ON FIRE" was first published in *War Crimes Against the Uterus* from Wide Eyes Publishing

"Becoming the Lilliputian" appeared in *Poke* from *Pink Plastic House*

"i started using a menstrual cup and this cycle has been different" & "ECHO (echo)" both appeared in the Spring 2021 anthology of Sunday Mornings at the River

"Kinks" was first published with *Prometheus Dreaming* as well as in *Memory* from *Tiny Spoon*

"Where It Hurts" also appeared in *Memory* from *Tiny Spoon*

"Weeds" appeared in Issue 6 of *Persephone's Daughters*

"but the moth sheds the caterpillar's fangs" was first published by Dark 30 Publishing and subsequently by *InHerSpace*

"A Poem in Which I Talk to Myself Just Like All of the Others", "D&C", "CamBaby" "I'll burn my own funeral pyre", & "Birth As a Trauma" are forthoming with *Bullshit Lit*

The following pieces were all included in the collection *Godshots Wanted: Apply Within* from Sunday Mornings at the River—

False Advertising
Something Black & Blue
why i'll always be haunted
16
ECHO (echo)
Weeds
Please, Take Your Ghost From My Son

···about the author···

Emily Perkovich is from the Chicago-land area. She is the Editor in Chief of Querencia Press, an art evaluator with Persephone's Daughters, and on the Women in Leadership Advisory Board with Valparaiso University. Her work strives to erase the stigma surrounding trauma victims and their responses. Her piece *This is Performance-Art* was a finalist for the 50th New Millennium Writings Award and she is a 2021 Best of the Net nominee. She is previously published with *Harness Magazine*, *Coffin Bell Journal*, and *Awakened Voices* among others. She is the author of the poetry collection *Godshots Wanted: Apply Within* and the novella *Swallow*. Her chapbook *The Number 12 Looks Just Like You* is forthcoming from Finishing Line Press. You can find her on IG @undermeyou or on Twitter @emily_perkovich

author photo first published with Suicide Girls©